Lost Century Compendium

Sherm Davis

LOST CENTURY COMPENDIUM:

POETRYPROSEPLAYSPIECES 1992-2001

SHERM DAVIS

SWIM (1994)	5
FLIRTING WITH NEPTUNE (1995)	49
UNDER ONE ROOF (1995)	111
SAN FRANCISCO POEMS (1999)	131
INTERNAL MEDICINE (2000)	141
TACITURN (2001)	181

SWIM

SWIM

TO ALL MY WHITE BROTHERS & SISTERS	9
BEYOND THE FALLOUT- A CENTO*	10
HAIKU	11
FRONT PORCH SUNDAY	12
HAIKU	20
MANIFESTO	21
UPON LANDING BEYOND KNOWLEDGE	22
THE SWORDED TAIL OF SWEET CHINA MIDNIGHT (PART I)	23
RELATIVITY	26
HAIKU	27
ON TRANSITS	28
SOMNAMBULATION	29
A WORD FROM OUR SPONSOR	30
HAIKU	31
CLOSEST THING	32
SWEET CHINA MIDNIGHT (SLIGHT RETURN)	34
THE RABBI & ME	36
WONDERLAND	38
HAIKU	39
SO YOU WANTED A FIRST PAGE	40
ON THE FUNCTION OF LINE (1995)	41
MORNING POEM	43
FOR ANDREW - BECAUSE YOU REALLY WANTED TO KNOW	44

To all my white brothers & sisters
(for Sonia Sanchez)

Wake up/sigh
blowdry yo hair
clench yo fist
and march/into
the bleakness of yo tomorrow
      (that will be $16.71 please)
and the anonymity of yo heritage.

Why you got holes in yo
pretty little dress girl?
i know momma wd freak
      she saw you aksin fo change
          stinkin like some crazy niggah wid
                blond dreads and
            the world shit on me
                    attitude.

Wake up/sigh
eat vegetarian maybe but
you still a cannibal
      razorblades in yo/eyes
          and stutters in yo smile.

Why you got holes in yo
pretty little nose girl?
      you white hindu 5-armed
        firebreathing marshmallow
            scared like you on the winning end/or
            somethin

BEYOND THE FALLOUT - a cento*

On Brooklyn Bridge I saw a man drop dead
It meant no more than if he were a sparrow.

The reason is obvious -- the large
cutbacks in social spending.
We aren't
except biologically mother
& son of course.

In the beginning
the energy between lovers may seem
chaotic & happening
Between any 2 points of bodily contact.

This is a book about extraterrestrials.

From 1919 on
food requisitioning was organized
and I have considered
enough of the cases to prove that
natural selection is incompetent thus
the mental model must
be seen not
as
a
static
library
of
images

Our young, rookie species
has recently passed through
several stages of intelligence

Mapping & colonizing the next frontier.

Haiku #1

Bright orange hunter
wander please into the range
of my fountain pen

FRONT PORCH SUNDAY

From my front porch

    I stare/a cosmonaut

        descended, listening

            to sounds of courting birds

        whose names I

    sometimes

        wish I knew.

So far from rice balls baked

    to perfection at Nino's on

        the corner of Union & Henry.

    And would three generations

        of Mazzolas work so hard perfecting

    if they could look & listen from my front porch?

II.

In my white plastic chair

        contemplating Jung's overexertion.

    My teeth have just been flossed

            and I dream of courting my

lover

      graceful

           sweet like the

     bird

        on

           my

              awning/i

dream of having

      no

        name

just a nest in Trinidad

      and your song to

           chase after.

III.

Breathing in & out. Looking at the three holes in my left sneaker

IV.

Once in

  Jerome

    Arizona

 after i

 ditched my hitcher

Went in for a beer/heard the music/gravitated/navigated my way round

  three Irish setters standing sentinel by the bar

   and

   there

   he

   was.

Have you ever heard a one-string washtub player

walk a bass line?

He sipped beer thru some/hidden

straw in his beard

tipped his hat when he

     caught me staring.

By the time

     the set was done I'd

          pumped five beers into my stuttering self
and

     crawled

         to

          his feet.

Teach me I begged

Teach me your walk

     your ear

     your eye

     how to cook

Strap me on your Harley and
        let's ride up the canyon and...

He handed me a pipe and said

      "Son, see these people?
      Today here's Labor Day --
      the one weekend we
      come out of prayer/ordinary and
      entertain."

He sipped his beard.

      "To you I might look like holy jesus or some
      ragged Joan of Arc but I'm Ted and
      every Labor Day I get a request just like yours."

I spit forlornly and rubbed my foot in the ground.

      "You must be one of them college poets or
      something," he laughed. "Come back tomorrow
      night if you want to work.
    And thanks for giving my cousin that ride
from Kingman."

V.

In Old Jerusalem where foot-smoothed stones
       crack my sandaled heels lives
             the harpist with whom I spent my late afternoons.

His white beard mocked me but I would not succumb to fear.
      He built his own harp/10 strings tuned like David's
      but I wouldn't let him scare me.

Four times he made me repeat the blessing for
    washing the hands before I stopped stuttering
        and the fifth time I stuttered on purpose just to see.

He laughed and we talked of god's nature

    we and it and indivisibility

    and he told me his story

    he shared with me history.

It was 16 Tammuz and approaching sunset,
and just as I was asking if I could spend the
holiday with him, maybe a second before,
      he opened the door, smiled and said,

      "Moses was slow of speech, David,
      and even he dropped the tablets of the law."

VI.

I lived a fairy tale once

middle winter

        highway 90

overheated   hitched to

Drummond, MT.

met a man/saved my life

        don't want to talk about it

suffice it to say

    cold only becomes real when you

lose the power of expression.

VII.

You & me

holding hands on a

Front Porch Sunday.

Haiku #2

I woke from ego's
dreams of fame and thanked my dad
for a common name.

MANIFESTO

"Love thy neighbor as thyself. All else is corollary. Now go study."
> — Rabbi Hillel, 1st century B.C.E.

Upon Landing Beyond Knowledge

was up late one night scribbling

poems my pen would never understand.

As with all moments of clarity, there was nowhere to begin.

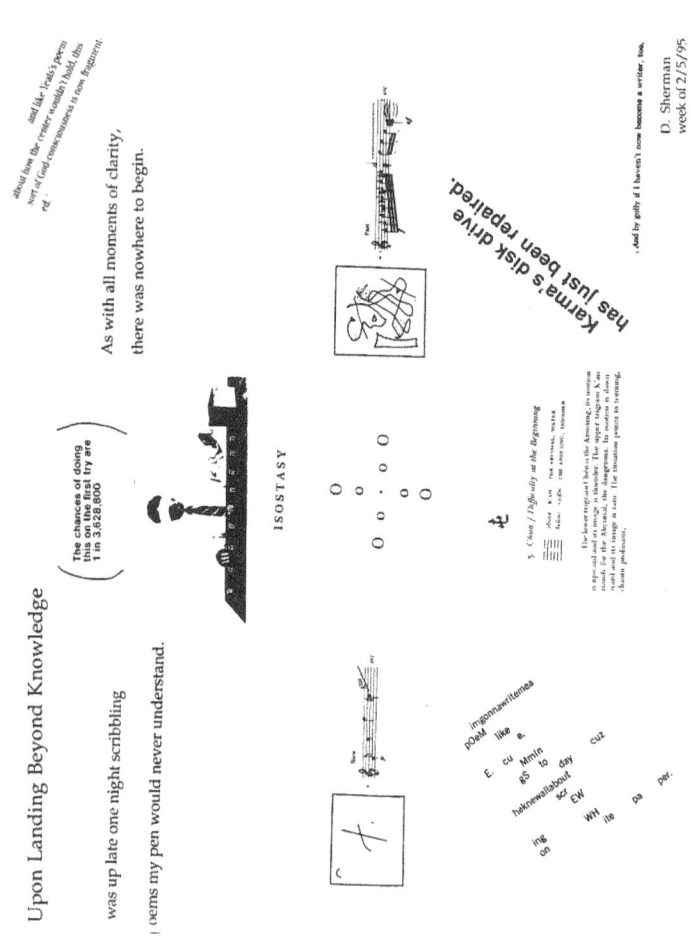

D. Sherman
week of 2/5/95

The Sworded Tail of Sweet China Midnight (Part I)

A string of pearls
>   Sweet China Midnight
>>   just another episode/postponing
>>>   my apocalypse one more day.

Be my magnet
>   *somewhere to hide when*
>>   *night becomes perpetual twilight/traces*
>>   *withering stars sliding*
>>>   *down a uranium sky.*

>>   *When the deer choke their final protest/shouting*
>   *"Hunt me/hit me with your car but*
don't let me go like this."

"I love the way you worry,"
>   China teased, tonguing
>>   her margarita glass.
"When you gonna get over your mother?"
>   She deposited a few
>>   salt crystals under my
>>>   nose with her tongue
and for a second I just wanted to stab her.

El Al Flight 101
>   *Non-stop New York to Tel Aviv*
>>   *In case of loss in cabin pressure put a mask on*
>>>   *yourself first, then your child.*
>   *Thank you for flying El Al.*

Thank me when we land/I said
>*to the second-year med student on my left.*
>>*She shared Rachmaninoff one ear each as*
>>>*we talked in hushed tones about*
>>*half-finished crosswords in*
>>>*airplane magazines and*
>>>>*Vidalia onions in Georgia.*

Can't talk too loud. Have to respect the Hasids
>*praying/12 hours straight.*
>*The plane might crash without them.*

"You used to be so much fun," China said,
>smelling the hate in my eyes.
>>"Let's go uptown. We'll hit the
>>Upper East Side and laugh at
>>all the clones and the misfits and
>>even **you** can't not have a good time."

"For an American you really don't speak so poorly," I said,
>knowing my joke went right on by.
>>I do that now & again with China.
>>>When her sex becomes too much
>>or I can't keep up with her sense of
adventure I
>resort to calling her
>>on
>>>her
>>>>syntax.

So it goes.

57 th street. Something like that. West Side near the river.
*   Walking home from the copyright office and a*
*   2 hour chat with an aspiring type.*
"Coke? Smoke?"
*   Where are you lady? Blended in with the bricks*
*   just your yellow eyes fireflies lust flicker.*
*   Oh. There you are.*
I sat. She rolled it and we
    watched
        the cops go by.
"No rock, lady."
    She put it away and smiled.
"You ain't a fool, boy."

No, lady, I ain't a fool.
    I sat with you cuz
        I know you're somebody's grandmother and
            we all can't be lucky enough to
                retire to Florida.

Relativity

My conundrum

    stems from your dilemma

        which derives in principle

           from my quandary

Your palindrome surfs wings across my oxymoron

    and I stutter indeterminately

```
                         how
                But              can
                                 yo
                                 u
                         be
                         so

                         su
                         re
```

Haiku #3

I see in those eyes
remnants of two world wars
and matzoball soup.

On Transits

For two holy weeks
Your moon splashed my life.
Fertilized my barren dreams.
For a little while there I was
      waking up before noon,
           forgetting the law of Karmic Return.
Now I talk to my Grape-nuts and squeeze
      banana-tomato juice by hand.
And you were right once when you said
No one ever sees what's
behind an eclipse.

Somnambulation

thru all my walks
thru 24-hour torture chambers empty buses &
      fast food restaurants
               half asleep & parched
I know I'm just another overtired
          overfed
          undernourished
          overprivileged
          underdisciplined
          overeducated
theoretically unjustifiably ignorant scamp trying
oh so hard to grasp at it while deepdown knowing
no matter what I do no news will make the headlines
no vitamins will miraculously turn up in our foods
what I'm really trying to say is I'm just another
sleepwalker.

A Word From Our Sponsor

I am fear. I am an active yogurt culture replicating in the caverns of your brain.   Ooze.
I am fear. I ride on your shoulder and whisper my weightless warnings wooingly.
I slogger around in the back of your throat and squeeeeeze when you allow me.
I am fear. A parasite suctioned to your small intestine eating the crumbs off the fingers of your urinary tract.
Are you ready for dinner?

Haiku #4

Zorro and Blackbeard
amateur swashbucklers as
compared to we two

closest thing
>   for Bukowski

Just another
tale of another
collapse

nothing to get
too alarmed about.
If you don't
want to listen
you can always
>   close the book
>   change the channel
>   flip the tape
>   pitch the bottle

No real reason you should
listen other than maybe
I took the time
to write this

Don't worry
I don't
expect you to

I'll still be here
at this blue
typewriter stabbing
trying to overcome my
nasty little habits

I do not write this
for you wherever or
whenever you are
I write this because
my blue typewriter talks
closest thing to
seductive whisper
ever crossed my ears.

Sweet China Midnight (Slight Return)

We got back to the apartment. F Train's always fun
at that hour. No night stop at Carroll so we went
three stops beyond and walked it back silently.
China doesn't like Brooklyn. Says it reminds her of
documentaries. My cousin was in Puerto Rico and
he left me enough to last the weekend. I turned on
the radio and sunk into the couch. She went into the
kitchen and started opening the cabinets. I lit the pipe.
Good shit.

> *Don't you still like me*
> > *she pandered*
> > > *stripping to her bra & panties*

Come on
> *Put your jewish cock inside me and tell me*
> > *the name*
> > > *of every*
> > > > *star in the sky.*

> *China relax i said*
> > *but she tackled my knees and*
> > *bit my shoulder*
> > *sliding blood over*
> > > *purple*
> > > *amphibian*
> > > *tongue*

*I was pinned jaws under hips
but determined to make my point*

*Let's just talk and listen to Thelonious
or smoke and drift
to sleep Sweet China.
It's only sunrise and you know
if we start now i'll be
asleep by 8 o'clock.*

*Apparently China didn't think this was
very funny/she took a glass from my
cousin's wine set and threw it/i ducked
but it hit me anyway and now my head
was bleeding along with my shoulder.*

*So i'm in hysterics now sitting in the
shower pouring peroxide
into my cut/my head is foaming i'm
screaming for attention*

I hear a crash of plates and a starlet scream. China comes out all hips and nasal in that ridiculous yellow hat holding three pieces of a coffee mug.
"Just plates and soy sauce. Don't you even have any leftovers?"

The Rabbi & Me

i heard the rabbi say now that you're here you see the plight of the people now that you're here you know. you can't hear the shells but you know
that
               they're
                           there

and you can't hear the air raid sirens but you know that
               they're
                           there

and that's enough to get you out of bed in the morning to walk to the Ko-tel and bend your knees and commune with the lord and is there anything for you still in the states is there anything but the bleak hope of fame and dinner parties and scores of unqualified journalists making comments about your apparel on Oscar night?
the rabbi said i will show you how to pray when you know that you will understand why we have persevered while everyone else disappears

i said what about brotherhood and what about we jews being a light for all nations and shouldn't we at least hear what they have to say i mean it's only the courteous thing to do we could learn from what they have to say too because there's more than one answer on this plague infested planet and though we may have gotten the word direct and i do believe we did they have taught me some things as well.

the rabbi said son this is Israel now forget your
American Superculture Mishmosh of every
conceivable religion and no discipline and MTV beach
parties and surrogate realities i'm talking about the
Book
of
Life
       and you want to be inscribed in the
Book
of
Life
don't you and i said yes
but why is there only one book
and do you need a credit card to apply?

Wonderland

Hatter came over yesterday and wishing Joan Armtarding

I've been thru all that said, "I just got a new potion hooked up with it days yesterday have even lent n

just get me a cup of tea.

Haiku #5

*You talked in your sleep
of angels and among them
you mentioned my name.*

So You Wanted a First Page

I wrote you a poem my love.
I sat down at my typewriter and really
struggled this time I didn't just
say the first thing that came to mind.
I typed page after page and ripped them out and tore
them up and never thought I'd
get finished but I did and
In my exhilaration I ran out the door with no shoes on
to show you my poem but I didn't realize eight inches
of snow had fallen and I was a little tipsy and I slipped
and the poem went flying into the street.
One page got hit by a car
but I saved it/you should have seen me
scrambling down Quail Street after my poem I
rounded it all up but I lost the first page. Here it is.
I have to go home now.

ON THE FUNCTION OF LINE (1995)

Frustration Poem

How strange it is
not to want anything
nothing to transmute
in either direction
it all just is

How strange
it is not to want anything
nothing to transmute
in either direction
it all just is

How strange it is not to
want anything nothing to
transmute it all
just is

How
strange
it is
 not
to want
 anything
nothing
to transmute
it
all
just
is

How strange it is not to want
anything nothing to transmute
it all just is

How strange
    it is not
        to want anything/nothing
    to transmute it
all just is (in either direction)

How strange
   it is not   to want anything
      Nothing to transmute in either direction
it all just is

How
strange it is
not to want any
thing no
thing
to transmute in either direction
it
all just
is

How strange it is not to want anything nothing to transmute in either
direction it all just is

How strange it is not to want anything nothing
to transmute in
either direction
it all
just
i
s

How strange it is not
              t
              o
              w
              an
              t anything nothing t
                                  o
                                  t
                                  r   d it all just
                                  a   i   i
                                  n   r   s
                                  s   e
                                  m   c
                                  u   t
                                  t   i
                                  e in either n

How strange it is not to want anything nothing
si tsuj lla ti noitcerid rentie ni etumsnart ot

h s i i
o t t s   not to want a   n
w r   n   o
    a   e   y   t
    n   t   t   h
    g   u   i   h   i
    e   to t^raⁿs^m   t   i_n g
                           j_{us}t a_ll
                                   i_s

etc.

Morning poem

predetermined afterglow
        sick on sweet wine

your mahogany 12-string
        dissonant against the sunstreaked sky

For Andrew -- because you really wanted to know

Janie was leaving for Key West. We'd been seeing each other for about three months when she told me she was leaving.

"Do you want anything?" she asked like another woman determined to shake the ills of another mediocre relationship by traveling to someplace she once heard was relatively exotic. There were days when Janie would wear a black and green and red and purple floral arrangement without a bra and her breasts would dance like feathers plunging over cliffs. This was one of those days.

"I'd really like a seashell," I said. "And maybe that pair of underpants as a souvenir."

Let me just say that I never wanted to write a story about underpants. Frank Zappa's already broached the subject with asymptotic fervency, superhuman tenacity, and there's little else that needs to be said; but Janie's were something special. Her mother must have bought them and given them to Janie because she didn't want to wear them. I don't know. I saw Janie's mother once -- it was June and her mother had come to Colorado to escape the oppression and the putrefaction of Louisiana. She was beautiful. A smaller, more resistant version of Janie that twinkled with the wisdom of a few more years and a few more husbands. I asked Janie if her mother was married right now. She cracked up. She never could tell when I was joking and when I was serious.

When we first made love at my place it was snowing and I seductively stripped because sometimes I'm a big shot like that, and Janie pulled her dress off vertically. Girding her hips was the most blessed weave of what appeared to be neoprene, khaki, wool and rayon. They were marbly white and green, a modern manufacturing miracle containing my

Janie as she performed her leadfooted version of a mating dance. It didn't matter. I wasn't looking at her feet.

She went to the bathroom and I took the aforementioned undergarments in my hands, feeling their texture, marveling at their construction. I hid them with hopes that she would leave them here and I could study them unobstructed by Janie's endless desire.

She came back from the john and as if linked by some internal homing device walked straight to the back of my closet and pulled them on without saying a word. She covered herself with all those crazy flowers and asked me to take her home.

When I saw her again the flowers must have all wilted because she was wearing a white sweater and a denim skirt. We went back to my place and this time I was Edward G. Robinson, talking out of the side of my mouth and waiting for her to come to me. She rubbed her breasts against my neck and unbuttoned her skirt. I was on the verge of seizure, drooling at the thought of those white and green neoprene khaki wool and rayon steel belted underpants revealing themselves to me in all their multinational splendor. (I actually looked it up – the underwear was a joint venture by The Soviet Union and the government of Sudan. During the Cuban Missile Crisis the designers were looking for a blend to survive nuclear fallout while still remaining comfortable and yielding maximal support. This was the alternate selection. The winners may be the topic of another story, some other day.) I imagined Janie stationed in Kamchatka or Yakutsk, just off the tip of Alaska, naked in the 60 below tundra except for her neoprenes, fighting off the invading blue Roman numerals with a rusty cannon and a pair of dice.

I finally got her skirt off and much to my chagrin made my way toward a pair of red and green and purple and black V-cuts. So that's where all the flowers went.

The reconstituted arrangement highlighted just the right amount of pubic hair, but my disappointed eyes had seen all that. Downheartedly imagining Sudanese agents knocking on Janie's door to confiscate her bloomies and Janie handing them over without a struggle, I lost my erection, and decided to just take her home. And I'm still waiting for that seashell to come in the mail.

SWIM WAS THE FINAL PROJECT FOR
ANDREW SCHELLING'S "WILD FORM"
FALL 1994, NAROPA INSTITUTE,
BOULDER, COLORADO.

*"BEYOND THE FALLOUT" IS A CENTO, A COLLAGE FORM, AND NONE OF THE WORDS ARE ORIGINAL OR COPYRIGHTED.

HELLO DAVE !!!!!!

Flirting with Neptune

FLIRTING WITH NEPTUNE

was completed in Boulder, Colorado, 1995

for Jim, who has inspired me more than he knows.

Flirting with Neptune

Chapter One: What Once Was Home
The Plainview-Brooklyn Shuttle

My Neighborhood/Verse for the Calling	55
Cadillac Man	56
Elf Child	57
Impression One -- exploded view	60
On History and the Subtle New Fascism	61

Chapter Two: Slate & Concrete
The Albany Years

Beverly Waverly, Wear & Share Your Rings	67
For Barbara, When She Wears Her Hair Down	68
Tibetan Man Runs the Hundred Meter in 9 Seconds	70
Of Acrobats & Prophylactics	72
Something Franklin Might Have Said	73
Confessions of Mild Wally's Employee	74
oh sister. oh sister nikki.	77
went incognito	79
Yo!!	80
Spiritual	82
Nihilism is a child's game	83
Cowboy Haiku	84
Not Until the Next Time	85
When My Feet Turn to Liquid	86

Chapter Three: Bittersweet Solitude
Bozeman, Montana

Rhyme for nikki	89
To a Step in a Particular Direction	90
Up on Ted Turner's Mountain	92
Pipe Dream #72	94
Article Appearing....	96
Parallel Haiku	97

Chapter Four: A New Pair of Eyes
The Boulder Experiment

Mallwalking	101
Supermarket	102
Lost Blue Library	103
When it rains	103
Lamentation of a Murderer	104
Jacob Haiku	105
Letter to K	106
try	107
Poem Against the Master's Degree	108
Affirmation	109

Chapter One:
What Once Was Home
The Plainview-Brooklyn Shuttle

My Neighborhood

Three coffee tables
   two toffee cables
      and a couple slabs o' wood
The Adels went to Tokyo to see America

A Haircraft Carrier flies by as fourteen
   little Japanese kids play on the Riemers' lawn.
Five quints, perhaps four twins -- the other nine look alike to me.
   Eight of those build trenches in the driveway
        (the other plays piano with me next door
         and listens to the commotion. She
         is fourteen and unblemished and her tiny almond
         eyes glitter as I improvise.
The haircraft carrier crashes down. Costner and Stallone
   Emerge and open fire on the Japanese kids. They
      climb into the trench and scream.
               The girl and I run outside to the trench and
She holds my hand, asking confusedly and in broken English
       what that thing is.
A HAIRCRAFT CARRIER
       I scream above the din.
WHAT?
A HAIRCRAFT CARRIER.
She shakes her head softly.

* * * * *

Verse for the Calling

As the unmarketable prophets
lie scattered in the street
The slap-happy idiot's
got new shoes on his feet

Cadillac man and his blue cloth roof
in the left lane drivin' blind
Renaissance man in therapy gloating
'bout the kids he left behind
Pizza man with anchovies
knockin' at my door
Sportscaster man on cable
tellin' me he knows the score

I'm not really angry
I know too much to get distressed
But when the glade ain't sprayed and the maid ain't paid
I sure can get depressed

Firebird man goin' 95
headlong into the rail
Schoolteacher pederast neurounstable man
gonna spend your life in jail
Alligator man in snakeskin
slither on outta here
Hair gel diamond stud mousse control man
buy me another beer

I'm not really all that upset
I've learned how to take it in stride
Until I find the mind I can unwind behind
in this kingdom I must hide.

Elf Child was disillusioned in Toyland. Though Mama and Papa Elf provided him every luxury, and reassured him nightly he was not an accident, Elf Child had no friends, and hurled hard-boiled eggs at anyone who came near him.

One Sunday when Mama and Papa Elf were praying to the Holy Elf of Spiritual Materialism, Elf Child stole the Maserati and took it for a spin.

He adjusted the pedals to suit his smallish (even by Elf Standards) frame and drove recklessly across the rocky plains. The buttes, mesas and barren, forbidding terrain took Elf Child's mind far away from the barricaded walls of his castle in the suburbs. He was filled with such elation that he failed to notice notice his foot grinding the pedal as far to the floor as his diminutive stature would allow.

When he finally turned his eyes to the road he saw the rear end of a large truck, and at 135 MPH swerved violently to avoid becoming Chicken Marsala. Tumbling off the road, Elf Child found himself pinned beneath the steering wheel, his head bleeding profusely.

Being an avid watcher of B-grade action movies, Elf Child knew he had to escape before the car exploded and the Museum of Natural History came for his skeleton.

Using tricks he learned on "Mr. Wizard's World" and "The Price is Right," Elf Child wriggled his way out of the twisted Maserati and ran towards the highway workers smoking cigarettes and building an imaginary drawbridge to protect the ice castle in the left lane.

He heard a sonic boom behind him, and involuntarily turned to look. As he turned a piece of shrapnel hurtled toward him and sheared off the tip of his nose, leaving a pug nose where a Roman once sniffed the wintry winds and the microwave pizzas of yonder yore.

The shock of this unanesthetized surgery sent Elf Child reeling -- right into the moat the highway workers were building around the imaginary drawbridge protecting the ice castle in the left lane. Very strange.

With his new nose, cranial hemophilia, retroactive amnesia and the surety that he was Wilford Brimley, Elf Child wandered through Phoenix, harassing pedestrians and forgetting to punctuate his sentences. One sentence in particular lasted seventeen hours.

Walking into a roadside diner to get a cup of coffee, Wilford read an article about a small (very small) child killed in an auto accident on a local highway. No remains were found, and the parents, local slaughterhouse moguls and holders of an exclusive corn remover patent, were distraught. He wrote down the address of The Church of Spiritual Materialism, finished his coffee, and went to pay his condolences.

Halfway down the street he realized that the vulgar sounding tirade in a mixture of some Slavic language and Chinese was directed at him -- he had walked out on a 55 cent check.

"Call my agent!" Wilford screamed, and spat at the little immigrant.

Strolling toward the church, he fondly recalled his days before stardom, when he spun plates on his nose and groomed the Maharishi's poodle.

The preacher didn't like Elf Child much, but because his parents had always donated generously, he prepared a wonderful eulogy dripping with admiration and 10-letter words.

The mass was quiet. Only two uncles and a schoolteacher with a twin fetish came to mourn the empty casket. The three made a date to go to the races after the funeral. You blame them?

A solemn Brimley dejectedly walked over to the parents, and in his most earnest voice said, "There, there. Don't cry. I brought you some oatmeal."

Mama Elf fainted. Papa Elf slapped his wayward son, and sent him to his room.

Impression One -- exploded view

    your hair is black but your eyes are purple. Staying up late to be his punching bag and letting him caress your bruised nipples with his tongue.
    you can't see me but i'm peeking through your keyhole and i'm watching your eyes making your body surrender.
    you'd rather die than be alone
    mama didn't train you for loneliness and papa just strokes your hair and remembers when you idolized him and vowed to love him forever and ever.
    but you're battered and beaten and your man won't stroke you like your daddy used to. No.
    he works late drinks and comes home and rides you till he's done and leaves you in a trash heap at the foot of the bed. Then he grumbles his undying admiration (i admire your steadfast refusal to quit also) and falls asleep.
    i know you're looking for me when you pray to the bug-stained ceiling. And i know you have no idea i'm watching.

On History and The Subtle New Fascism

Reaching back
to a day when all my cares rested snugly between
A New York Yankee and King Arthur's court
And golddiggers plundering new frontiers, staking their claims,
Proclaiming their divinity.

American by birth, yet still searching for that homeland
       promised me when I took
              that Pledge of Allegiance.
       Or maybe just looking for an America
             within
              these
              borders
              a land of the free (look at the Navajo)
                            a home of the brave (look at the Hopi).

Through rain through hail through sleet through Brooklyn
Grandpa served the red white & blue.
Through presidents and failed regimes and
Grandma's matzoball soup
He upheld the dignity his profession required.

He swam with Weismuller.
If handball had been an Olympic sport he'd be a
       household name.
He did the Times crossword in ink and let me chew his
       cigars through the plastic.

Fifty some-odd years and a federal pension later
he doesn't even recognize a Scrabble board.

No saturated fats
        or salt
        or sweets
        or brownies
        or wine
        or red meat

his doctor said twenty-five years ago,
And he upheld the dignity his profession required.

Sure, American medicine can bombard us with statistics,
take over our newspapers, lengthen our pitiful lives by years.
But what can Grandpa do in his second infancy?
He can complain to Grandma (who statistically will
        outlive him by 2.7 years) or he can go to a
Bright and shiny nursing home
and eat tasteless mashed potatoes and
have his diapers changed by sterile nurses.

Or he can just stare at the wall.

The '27 Yankees and the golddiggers of the
        Old West lived by
        different rules.
Though they knew they were conquerors they
        believed in their cause.

They'd sew their own wounds, meet their
fate behind a cloud of
      tobacco or a bottle of moonshine --
      So maybe disease ran rampant. False hope did not.

If I ever see Grandpa again I'm going to take him out for a
      big
            juicy
                  burger.

Chapter Two:
Slate & Concrete
The Albany Years

Beverly Waverly, Wear and Share Your Rings

Tick Tick
Frantic Syncopation
In Double-Breasted Tweed
Stuttering Heart
A Cellophane Goldfish
Choking On Air.
My Cleopatra, So Long and Wispy
Dark and Supple
I Stand Sole Sentinel
Waiting for Dawn to Arrive.

For Barbara, When She Wears Her Hair Down

You showed me Sonia
And June and Cliff
And for a moment -- one moment
      I left my scarlet begonias
            to take a whiff/of your
bony black sweat and patchouli perfume
as it cascaded cross
those
      tiny
            desks
                  that separated
you from me.

You called me white and adjusted your glasses
as a fragile smile parted your delicate lips.

But I see you in your silver skirts preachin'
      for your people.
I even once heard
      some semblance of a sequestered soul
Crack that coifed composure.

Then it was my turn to smile.

Slip up and lose it, go on.
Academia's accusatory accent
      never did suit your
           frail and timid strength.

But don't you dare stand up there and
      tell me you understand.
You're too sexy
      well-dressed
      polished and pedicured Barbara
Vegetarian rewriting history.
You call it sewage but this white boy call it shit.
Go on home to Georgia Love,
And don't you ever come back again.

~~*

TIBETAN MAN RUNS THE HUNDRED METER IN 9 SECONDS!

The New World

I read in the paper today that man is
soaring to brave new heights.
Codons crumbling hurricanes levelling Pensacola.
What would good old Aldous say today
if he were to walk down the aisles of a Minneapolis Safeway?
Would he buy those three cans of tuna fish
      a waxy apple
        Monsanto milk and Calgene tomatoes?

The Holy Land

Ho ho ho and away we go
  health insurance prozac
    good for mommy daddy
    ritalin for the kids.

Stabilize me pump me full
  of your funky bass beat kicking up dirt
  on a new Jerusalem street
let me drown in decay in the sweltering heat
let me rhyme so sublime let me sit in your seat.

there's nothing holy
      left
         to
            write
and

there really isn't too much left to figure out. So
when the last novel is written
    (and most of my friends think it has been)
Will Chaucer just be another astrologer gone mad?

Coda: Himalaya Suite (Colorado '95)

High up here the pilgrims seem so little.
Trudging up and up in their Saabs and wondering
if these mountains really were constructed in 1931
or whether that photographer was having himself a joke.

~~*

Of Acrobats and Prophylactics

In spurts it comes
Yes we all do know that
But the hat that's the hardest
      it is worn by the acrobat
Trapezing so breezy and
Wheezing so easy and
Sneezing so sleazy and
Barely the know-how to make it all rhyme!
But the acrobat growing fat making plans with the diplomat
Shaking hands with the hardhat, a sycophantic bureaucrat,
Wiped his feet on the doormat squashed the mantis
      with a big splat.
Know what he spat after that?
"Oh drat! Oh drat!"

SOMETHING FRANKLIN MIGHT HAVE SAID

To sleep is righteous if you've earned your rest
Rain is sacred when the lava flows red
Gods are righteous if your soul's content
Dogs never mind when you long for a friend
Poetry is solace to the wounded heart
Prose is the refugee's bride
The play is the spout of the desperate shout
of the warrior's waterlogged pride.

Confessions of a Mild Wally's Employee

Last summer I had the privilege of passing through the golden portals of everyday existence, to transcend, if such a word can be used to define an anchovy and a chef's salad, into the Wonderful World of Wally. "What was it like?" you may ask. Well I, the delusional writer without a twopence in my pocket, wandered into Wally's one warbling Wednesday, weary and waylaid, desperately needing cash. In a purple tank top and lewd cut-off shorts I begged, and my prayers were answered.

Rob, the boss, the master of the sarcastic reply, balding, wearing white puffy chef's hats on alternate Thursdays, asked me if I had any pizza experience. "Yes, Robert, I do," I replied. "I worked for Pizza Hut as a delivery driver and I quit because I could no longer be held down by fascist Neo-Nazi cartoon characters who lacked the intelligence to type their own names into the grand old computer terminal. Besides, they made me shave."

Well, Rob chuckled a bit and said, "Son, you're just the demented convoluted young sailor Wally has been looking for. Here's my beeper number. Wake me tomorrow at 9:30 and be in at ten." We shook hands in that same sardonic manner and I knew this was the place for me. That night I was so excited I stayed out till 5:30 drooling on myself. At 9:20 my alarm woke me. I called Rob and dragged my sorry ass to work at 10:15. When I got there Barry, Wally's other hired hand, was still asleep in the basement. This palatial estate consisted of an aging mattress sandwiched comfortably between a meat case and a freezer. Ah, this was home!

Quickly I became adept at taking the phone off the receiver and greeting the awaiting customer with a languid hullo. Within two weeks, I was learning how to use the calculator! Did the guys love me! They made me a driver, and sent me everywhere! Whether it was Loudonville or Schenectady, or the napkin supplier or the cheese warehouse, they sent Dependable Dave. Every morning I would wake Rob, careful not to disturb Barry sleeping in the palace once I got to work. Boy did I learn the tricks quick! If I had to make five chef's salads, I'd make only two of them wrong! But at Wally's that didn't matter. Their motto was, "ANY BUSINESS IS GOOD BUSINESS."

They had a few regular customers, don't get me wrong. Every morning I knew I'd be taking a ride to Finnegan's, the Greek store, and to this one lady named Anna Jane who lived on the sixth floor of the Albany Psychiatric Center. She was so nice. She'd always smile so sweetly and soothingly and say, "You're that cute little boy from Uncle Phil's, aren't you?" And then she'd break down on my shoulder and tell me about this horrible uncle she had when she was a kid who used to call her Sweet Pookums and play fire engines with her. It became quite a ritual.

But business was slow, summer mornings at 97 degrees not being the most opportune time to order a scalding hot pizza, so I took the time to acquaint myself with the other delusional idiots I was sharing sanctum with. We had a ball. This one dude Mike, a really hip black guy in his late thirties, knew the words to every song on Oldies 99.5. He and I spent the mornings discussing the end of the world and the astrological significance of palindromic years. We had a special peace sign we would flash if either Rob or King Barry would lose their heads over something stupid like us spilling a container of vegetable oil down the stairs. And we ate. Mike and I really ate. It's not like we made subs, or wings, or anything time consuming. We'd peek in to the freezer and take roast beef, just one or two slices, out of the container. We'd drink three iced teas in a row just to see if we could. This was quality time.

But the first signs of my demise in this realm of the work force came at just about the time the phones started ringing again in late August. Mike had long since been canned, basically because they suspected him of doing all the damage, and I was too poor to take the rap for him. Hauling 75-pound cartons of cheese just wasn't the same anymore. Signing my name on their bills just lost all its twinkle, and after awhile I just wanted to go down to the basement and sleep.

*****

oh sister. oh sister nikki

Give to yourself
before you reach out and
feel free as
wind at thirty knots
in my stomach as I
share acid of your ulcer and
wrenches of your longing.
Let me not invade your
private holy sacred space but instead bask
in shared light and
let me improvise on your skin but
say No if No is
what you mean.
My voice, (la-la-la-locked be-behind
ffffear and stuttering) mayhem's child
changing insecurity's curtains.
Reverse polarity my handy excuse.
Let me not invade no not invade.
Stand like a sentinel maybe but
not invade no
But help you to help me to help you BREAK DOWN
learned myths and learned helplessness.
BREAK DOWN roles and rules not to hedonism
Nor anarchy (though that would be nice)
but unadulterated streams of thought.
Nikki my voice is so close but not touching
yours it is locked in my throat to wriggle
wrestle its way out.
Help me stare me in the eye
Melt me BREAK DOWN please but
share and no more acid and no more
Death maybe aging but aging happily

Do you understand? Do I ask too much?
Yes I do so
I will not just
show me what lingers
I know I spit and shit and spout
but I try to get it out although
it looks like heaps on porcelain floors.
Yellow light I feel when you
hold me.

II

I could be high and
happy and
smiling like Clark Kent
behind glasses and flying
like him too
over disfigured cities
turning back
Time for Love
Oh Lovely Lois
If i c-c-c-could
If i c-c-c-c-could
 if i if i
 if i if i
c
c
c
c
could
       only
             spit
                    it
                          out

                                          Aah.

Went incognito
Didn't want to be beautiful no more.
Wanted to see it from the poor man's side
But in this world you're bound to your caste

The flowers the clover patches
me them the onlookers
we all changed places

```
            high I looked out over the artillery gardens
     feet
     ten                              and
    be                                 I
   to
  grew                                         laughed
 I
```

for a moment
    at those
       peasant plants

            fighting for drops
            of
            rain

```
             . .
          .  .   .
        .  .  .   . .
          .      .    .
         .     .       .
       .    .     .      .
      .    .   .     .       .
    .    .      .      .    .    .
```

Yo!

Yo coppa
getcha hands off me
I didn't do nothin
but sing and yeah I sang
and you can't make me stop coppa
Throw my hands behind me touch me
    strip me coppa
lock me up yeah you coppa
But you can't touch me shake me
You dumb coppa
smilin hatred
to me cuz long hair and
happiness i EARNED yeah mothafucka
Earned by tears & scars & love you fuck
LOVE.
You kickin yoself fo dem choices you made?

Yo teach.
i back.
superstarstuddedstudentstraightasa
Arrow. Starts with A
A. A. All A.
Real good I did on yo tests teach
And you told me I was good.
yeah good. Made me smile teach.
You showed me 20-letter words
And 26 letters and countless permutations
And vacillations oscillations I felt using
    those endless combinations.
    Oh endless ations.

But teach them don't get me no mo.
don't do nothin
You teached me double meanings
And secrot words teach
now I feel like I am hiding
Tree letters a word and tree words a sentence.
Guilty not guilty.
And I plant one in yo rocky little head.

SPIRITUAL

Let the damned
wander faithless
but do not accept their sweets!
Let them builds palaces,
shrines,
mosaics of stone,
But look aloft!
For you lay low, now,
perhaps, but your day shall come!
Dig!
The illusion runs like the Nile.

My gypsy queen
can you hear me scream?
The rabid hunter shouted
to the vast noiseless Sphinx.
Dance all night
to Egyptian flames
and blazing salts
But do not look back,
for Lot had to lie with his daughters.

If you, Love, are of the Heavens,
then I am of the Earth,
doomed to wander and stumble,
eyeless and palsied,
awaiting celestial release.
But if you are of the Holy Fire,
come,
and may the cool spring wind
scatter our ashes Home.

Nihilism is a child's game.

Nihilism is a child's game.
Supplication
       flight
              quiescence television
          all spiritual excuses.
There is something to do
(the fool scratches his head)
But what?

Nothing.

Formative years and anorexic souls
locked in holding patterns,
spitting up altruism chiseling destiny and failure.
"Throw your honesty to the wind," my TV screams,
"Set your sails for home!"
But as hungry eyes sift through advertisements
       cheesy novels
       endless sitcoms
the reckless abandon of youthful days gives way
to stuttering confidence and metered prudence.
Steps step steeper
steeper
       and
              steeper
                      we step.
We walk Mercer's hill -- merciless
men throwing stones, cutting knees.
Caning our brothers/pillaging our sisters
Transmuting sex to anger/anger to sex.
Is it our hatred?
Jealousy?
Or have we just forgotten who we are?

**IF SPURS OF THE MO
MENT ARE ALL I CAN MUSTER
CALL ME COWBOY BOB**

Not Until the Next Time

I will never forget.
Not the beauty, nor the pain
The way I cherished your lips
And helped your bleeding heart cry.
The so seldom sunshine
the snow that sequestered
the sensuous September storms.
The psychic struggle
the bipolar disarray.

I will often rummage through
the attics of yesteryear,
laughing away tears I have too often cried.
I will mourn the beautiful ballerina
with ten broken toes
and the boy who died breathing her dance.

I will never for you write another line
nor let you swim in my ocean.
Never again will your name cross my lips
nor your harbor receive my ship.

Nor will your melancholy smile
haunt the waves of my beaches where
glittering suns once shined.

WHEN MY FEET TURN TO LIQUID

WHEN MY FEET TURN TO LIQUID AND MY ANKLES ARE CHAINED TO BIG HEAVY BALLS AND MY SHOES ARE TIED TOGETHER AND MY LEGS ONCE SO SUPPLE ARE GELATIN BLOBS AND MY PENIS WANTS ONLY TO CRAWL BACK INSIDE AND MY STOMACH IS SWISHING AND DANGLING AND MY ARMS FLANK MY SIDES LIKE THE DEADEST SEQUOIAS AND MY BEARD HANGS TO BY NIPPLES SO SUNKEN AND DRY AND MY HAIR IS A NEST FOR THE SPIDERS AND SPOOKS WHO SPIN DELICATE WEBS IN MY BRAIN I STRIP TO THE BONE AND WALK STRAIGHT TOWARD THE SUNSET AWAY FROM THE DOUBLE YELLOW LINE AND AFTER DAYS OF WALKING MY FEET ARE BLEEDING AND THE BONE IS PEEKING THROUGH BUT I WALK AND I FIND IT I COME TO THE SACRED ROCKS AND MY HEART SCREAMS AND CRIES I HAVE FINALLY FOUND IT I CLIMB UP THE ROCKS AS FAST AS I CAN I FEEL LIKE A MONKEY BUT I FALL AND CUT AND BLEED AND THE SUN BAKES MY SKIN AND DRIES MY BLOOD BEFORE I CAN DRINK IT I KEEP CLIMBING HIGHER AND HIGHER AND HIGHER NAKED AND HAIRY AND BLEEDING AND SMILING AND I GET TO THE TOP AND I YELL LIKE A SAVAGE AND I BEAT MY CHEST AND PULL MY BEARD AS WORDS BECOME SCREAMS AND EMOTIONS I CLOSE MY EYES AND RUN STRAIGHT OFF THE EDGE LAUGHING SINCERELY MERCILESSLY IN A VOICE THAT IS MINE I SPREAD MY ARMS AND SPREAD MY LEGS AND ARCH MY BACK AND JUST FALL AS SECONDS BECOME EPOCHS I SEE A MOVIE OF MY LIFE IN FAST FORWARD AND I CRY AND THANK MYSELF THAT I AM HERE FALLING.

Chapter Three: Bittersweet Solitude

Bozeman, Montana

Rhyme for Nikki

Dear nikki dear you haunt me clear
to the marrow of my bone.
For as long as I still have you
I'll feel mortally alone.

To a Step in a Particular Direction

Sometimes, gazing through the candlelight,
hiding behind the lamplight,
I glimpse a cross-section of your soul,
   a trick of the light off the curtains.
Delirious with pain and longing,
I contemplated writing you a crazed love letter,
   dripping with sorrow, begging for reaffirmation.
So I made some tea and lit a candle,
and here I am dancing with my dark side.

The Tarot gave me nothing new.
The Nine of Cups again my love.
Vacillation -- powerful currents if properly controlled,
highly destructive if left to roam free.
You are The Star, love, as always you have been.

They're developing that field across the way.
Remember that field? The one you used to stare at
through steam clouds rising from your
chamomile tea at sunset?
Some developer from Massachusetts who knows
Montana only through real estate listings and ski brochures
has decreed that the world needs another rec center or
home for the elderly.

I am leaving before the tractors come.

Old age calls me.
        Israel calls me.
                Salvation calls me.

And your call fades
	slowly dies
		in the fog.

I see you in his bed, scared, yet awakened by
	each new sensation.
And like a father waving goodbye I must just
	close the door
and know and trust the power with which I
	helped create you.

Up on Ted Turner's Mountain
        Bald eagles circle
                for the moment.
Buffalo roam the frozen plain
        Immune to gawking
                tourists passing through.
In the executive washroom
        at Channel Eight
The anchor powders her cheeks.
        Vultures roam the set as
Technicians read the new Danielle Steel
        between twenty-second video shoots.
The sun never shines
        But it really doesn't need to --
Turner's got it all under control.
Colorization: that's the key.
Never let them see you smile.
        Keep the perm soft, the contacts colored,
                the smile all plastered wide.

Up on Jane Fonda's operating table
        Doctors stand on call,
Two by two
Two by two
        to   pull   the   skin   tight
                as   soon as it sags.
In the front row in Atlanta,
        in the mezzanine on the moon,
She stands by her man, she sits by his hip,
        Someone's got to guard the wallet.
And Ted, oh, Ted, He's got quite
        a pretty woman, hey!! She can
Aerobicize with the best of 'em.

And I wonder how it got to be this way as I drive
Up on Ted Turner's mountain.

    I know where I stand --
    I can't be alone.
    Why does this sound like a question?

To uphold the mold you must be sold,
    You must be told, you can't be bold.
        You must be cold, eternally old,
            Ready to fold, to cash in your gold.
Have your virtues extolled, your constituents polled,
Up on Ted Turner's mountain.
    The ride is free, so much to see!
    Oh what you could have been
If you just took a right
    instead of a left
Up on Ted Turner's mountain.

Pipe Dream #72

Do I seem inattentive?
I'm so sorry.
Sometimes I think about the rain
in New Mexico and I cry.
Sometimes I wander through the ephemeral garden
and pick the berries.
And sometimes I just stare.

I met her today at the train station.
Her name was Rockxanna.
She showed me her passport, laughing at
the way official photographs always made her
look like her mother.
I (with 5 planets in Virgo) inquired about the
      triple consonant.
She smiled and said her mother wasn't much of a speller but
you should see her fix an engine.

Feathery black hair tied loosely in a barrette.
A 2-dime gap between her front teeth.
Melting I stood, grappling at conversation,
impressing myself actually with my waterline knowledge
of all kinds of meaningless subjects
      (compared to the hazel in her eyes).

Day drew on, we talked and talked.
I let my train go by, she just smiled and
      told stories of France, Portugal, and half-brothers
and sisters scattered like confetti through Europe.

Enraptured I stood, barely containing my drool.
The sun was sinking and spirit stood suspended,
and she talked about robbery in her basement apartment
and vacationing in Monaco!!
Arteries ruptured and spit blood on the tracks.
She took no notice at all.
So I patched myself up and tried to act casual.
And just before the sun sank behind the mountains,
the princess requested a grape juice.
And when I returned she was gone.

Article appearing in Rolling Stone magazine, February 30, 1993

Recently, an article appeared in a Stanford law journal entitled, *"Can a Family of Five Eat a Ton of Beef Per Week?"* The research, remarked Dr. Elliot Tingles, Professor at Law, was both meticulous and conclusive. Dr. Tingles agreed with the students that the average American family could consume a ton of beef per week, with no adverse effects on its health. In fact, the study went on to conclude that when taken with other vitamins in moderate doses, this diet would actually improve the subjects' overall well-being. And besides, those long dinners are quite conducive to familial conversation, between parents and their children, and between siblings.

When asked why the students chose a medically related article for their term paper, their spokesperson, Sharon Machiavelli, quipped, "the point we as students are making is that a well-phrased research paper need not be about anything substantial, nor even anything remotely beneficial to the common good." She then added, "But we got an A!"

The students were commended for their originality, their willingness to manipulate the rigid guidelines of the law program, and their ability to contort statistics while keenly staying within the parameters required by the professor.

In other words, Dr. Tingles rewarded the students for undermining the very principles for which he gave his life to teach. When asked to comment, Dr. Tingles replied, "Well, I've always liked red meat."

*Flying next to you
two parallel lines destined
never to connect*

Chapter Four:
A New Pair of Eyes
The Boulder Experiment

MALLWALKING

Locked and drowning
inside some adolescent version
        of misplaced Piscean projection
O winged pre-pubescent pseudo-angel
tell me of your acne-ridden sufferings.
That white cut shirt with vertical stripes isn't
supposed to hide those
emerging nipples and
growing sense of displacement.
Kali wears her tongue pierced
and you, pulled by ancestral tide,
stare through pot-glazed eyes.

And you, meditation lady dressed in black,
you snuck a peek at my aura, didn't you?
And you turned abruptly the other way.
You and your therapist friends think you know how
        to bring people from darkness to light.
But you have no idea how to handle clarity.

No lady, not again.
I've given you change three fucking times and still you
        don't recognize me.
So maybe it's not part of the job description to
look at your benefactors, but this time
you get your change from somebody else.

Supermarket

Wondering if this
vegetarian diet isn't
making me altogether
too sweet & unbearable
smiling at redheaded
cashier pretending
plutonium isn't
hibernating
8 miles
away.

Lost blue library
    Palace of wisdom and doom
        And things I'll never have time to know.
    Haven for scholars and quiet drunks wading
        Through ponds of fearful adolescent mystery.

Hear ye spiders and ceaseless warriors
    Crawling the aisles of time
        'tis a joyous day, come out and play.
    The sun is peeking boldly out
        From behind the mushroom cloud of history.

* * * * *

When it rains
I think of that Saturday
in Southampton we never had.

Lamentation of a Murderer
for O.J.

Three times I checked on you
before I dropped that axe through your head.

A Sunday morning
      birds still singing
           Venus still lingering above
the stucco stairs of your condominium complex.

I sat and watched the churchgoers, waited and watched.
Finally I ascended and knocked.
You didn't answer, but your car was in its assigned
parking space,
      and I know you never take the bus.

The second time I stalked you in my Nova.
You and he and a Mexican Hamburger stand.
I probably could have handled his $70 sunglasses, and
even his lamplight tan.
But when he order that strawberry frappe
and you looked at him like he was sophisticated
I knew I had no choice.

The third time was a simple phone call.
I just wanted to have you over for dinner.
"Jason and I aren't home right now. Please leave
your name and number and we'll get back to you just as
soon as we can.
Toodles!!"

**Toodles?
Toodles?!
Darling you could have saved so much unnecessary bloodshed if only
you hadn't said Toodles.**

* * * * *

Jacob haiku

THEY SHOULD WRITE HOLY

BOOKS ABOUT THE WAY YOU STOLE

AND SOLD MY BIRTHRIGHT

Letter to K

Standing over the ring of toilet
contemplating my roommate's pubic hair,
I squeeze my last few drops and
shake my head at this recurring predicament.

Pre-fab love you came to shame me,
showering sweet simulacrum/clarity's clone.
I would have loved you maybe but
you talk too much in your sleep and
too little when you're awake.
When I said I didn't like having sex with you
I only meant let's close the blinds
and cuddle for awhile.

try
to
picture
you
me
rejoicing
forgetting
the time
you
fucked
your
friend
the time
I
fucked
mine
for spite
and
the cycle repeated.
just imagine
for a
second
New Mexico
skies
cloudless
apotheosis
just
youandme
regretless
and free
indian
summer
chamomile tea
no more
alphabet
can you
visualize
that?

Poem Against the Master's Degree

another day
pictures on the wall
landscape the poet
language the imitator

roll with me celestially
the satyrs call our name
i'll inject you with my archer's bow
you'll prance the horse's softshoe and
we'll silence the linguists with
      geometric alliance
waterfalls cascading icosahedrons dancing

zero-gravity fellatio
that's the way I want to go

AFFIRMATION

In the dim light given us meekly
I see traces of an old footprint shine
In the miasma a song plays discreetly
In fear abysmal a blue flame still pines.
Its essence beyond doubt eternal
Its source the unfolding blue stream
Far past the cold flames infernal
To the light of the mystical dream.

Beyond meditative awareness
On through the vortex of night
A dream so complete in its bareness
Where dark is the essence of light.
Where paradox truly emerges
Where hate and love truly embrace
From Four Points the One Stream converges
Guiding us softly through Time and through Space.

10/17/94

Under One Roof

Works for Stage

Euripides in Hollywood
a fanciful rendition of the Bacchae

113

My Sweet Komachi
a varation on Noh Drama

119

Suspension
a play for two acrobats

127

"Under One Roof" contains the highlights of
Anne Waldman's workshop at Naropa Institute, Boulder,
Spring 1995.

Euripides in Hollywood

One Night Only: A Fanciful Rendition of The Bacchae

Characters:
Mataam Fez: Hollywood restaurateur, astrologer to the stars.
Leona Helmsley: Seriously wealthy woman. Mother of the future king.
Rupaul: Mortal, tempts & confuses the gods with his gender-bending antics.
Chorus: Rupaul's harem.
George Burns: god of winter.

The Myth:
When Leona Helmsley was pregnant, she had a feeling the kid would be something special. Opposed to ultrasound, she consulted Mataam Fez at his Moroccan restaurant for a horoscope of her unborn baby. Mr. Fez predicted the boy would become king, but that in a certain year (this one) he ran a great risk of being killed in a skiing accident. Hearing this, the wealthy Ms. Helmsley paid Rupaul a healthy ransom, and promised to make him Slumlord of Hollywood, if he and his harem could keep George Burns happy and occupied, thus keeping winter away. A deal was struck, and we join The Bacchae in progress, Third Episode, Choral Dialogue.

Third Episode, Choral Dialogue.

RUPAUL: Ho-o! Hullo!

> D'you hear me calling - hear my voice?
>
> Hullo, trannies, hullo gender-benders!

CHORUS: What is it? What is it? Where is this voice

> calling me from slumber?

RUPAUL: Hullo! Hullo! Hear me again:

> Sons of MTV! Daughters of Sid Vicious!

CHORUS: Master, our master! Ho, Hullo!

> Come dance with us, rave with us.
>
> Take ecstasy and shake with us!

RUPAUL: Androgynous Michael --

> Spirit of Hollywood, owner of the rights to
>
> Elvis and the Beatles -- rock the house!

CHORUS: Ah! Aah!

> The palace of George Burns shall soon come to ruin. No man his age can withstand our temptation! Our seduction!

FIRST VOICE: Yo! Rupaul is in the house!

SECOND VOICE: Turn down the bass! Let us hear our master speak.

RUPAUL: Temptation, seduction shall
> our weapons be, as we
> withhold the winter this year!
> And we will tussle with the gods,
> And emerge victorious!
> A feat no she-male has managed.
> And I will be the slumlord of Hollywood,
> And you will all be rich!

CHORUS: Aah! Aah!

    Look, d'you see the eyes gleaming

    When he makes his plans?

    The very fire his vision's breathing

    Bodes well for our future as actors.

    Fling yourself in supplication

    at the feet of the master.

RUPAUL: Come, my Oriental ladies --

    Have I frightened you so well

    You have fallen to the floor?

    You know my power, you know my agent,

    Do not be afraid to succeed.

    Come, get up and stop your trembling.

My Sweet Komachi

Variation on a theme from Noh Drama

PERSONS: A traveling priest (waki)

A fisherman (shite)

A woman (tsure)

TIME: Late autumn

WAKI

I have traveled by foot for many miles, and I am hungry. Do you have any fish for me to eat?

SHITE

Fish are all I have in this life. They are my home and my family. Take all you need.

WAKI

Thank you, sir. You are kind. Yet you seem lonely. Your eyes look but do not see beauty. I am a priest. Come, tell me your story.

SHITE

I will tell you.

(TSURE enters in a white robe -- music like shrill wind)

SHITE

Long ago -- too long, I was young and strong.
Noble not by birth but by heart. I was a poet.
My plays were played before the king.
I ate well, and had all my needs attended to.

TSURE

He was majestic

SHITE
Words flew from my pen, wit from my tongue. I do not exaggerate in old age.

TSURE
So handsome his wit!

SHITE
In the height of my career I met Komachi. She sang like a thrush in spring. But in late autumn no songs do I hear. Only fish, and more fish!

TSURE
Oh yes, I could sing!

(TSURE sings softly in the background)

SHITE
I loved Komachi, and she loved me so. We agreed to marry and set a night to be wed.

WAKI
This story does not sound sad at all!

SHITE
And never did it have to! My folly -- my youth. My indecision!

TSURE
He promised he would marry me!

(she continues singing)

SHITE
And then I decided my poetry should suffer were I to wed -- my contact with Muses diminished to one.

WAKI
One muse consistently seems to me more inspiration than to be at the whim of the Fates!

SHITE
Had I only seen! I was so young -- lost in the trance of my power. I had servants to bathe me, my audience kings. What did I need of a wife?

TSURE
The young poet with the world at his feet. Had only he thought once of his wife!

SHITE
The night is progressing but the moon is in hiding. Need I tell you the rest?

WAKI
No, you do not. I have heard quite enough. But may I ask of you just one more thing?

SHITE
Ask, please ask. I've nothing but time amongst these fish and this water.

WAKI
Did your beloved ever marry?

SHITE
Since the height of my youth I have not seen Komachi. Yet on nights with no moon her sweet soprano slips through my floorboards and keeps her memory close.
Come, good priest, I know you need lodgings. Spend the night in my cabin, and you too can hear my sweet Komachi sing.

(Exit SHITE and WAKI. TSURE sings her song and circles the pines.)

SUSPENSION
a play for two acrobats

running time 8 minutes 30 seconds

In the center of the stage sits a trampoline. On the trampoline sits a harness, wired wide at the shoulders to a pulley system above the stage. No attempt should be made to hide the wires. Suspended seven feet high, upstage left, is an OLD MAN in a harness, sitting crosslegged and blowing bubbles continuously with a wand and a jar. Spotlight on him at all times. A more diffuse light on the trampoline and center stage.

YOUNG MAN enters. Puts on harness. Waves frantically at OLD MAN. Gets on trampoline. Bounces twice. Jumps to floor. Waves frantically. Gets on trampoline. Bounces higher. Waves frantically. Jumps to floor. Waves frantically.

Gets on trampoline. Bounces higher. Waves frantically. Does backflip. Waves frantically. Jumps to floor. Waves frantically.

Gets on trampoline. Bounces higher. Waves frantically. Does backflip. Waves frantically. Reaches apex of jump and suspends momentarily, four feet high. Waves frantically. Falls to trampoline. Jumps to floor. Looks up at OLD MAN.

Gets on trampoline. Bounces higher. Waves frantically. Does backflip. Waves frantically. Reaches apex of jump and suspends momentarily, six feet high. Waves frantically. Falls to trampoline. Jumps to floor. Looks up at OLD MAN.

Gets on trampoline. Bounces higher. Waves frantically. Does backflip. Waves frantically. Reaches apex of jump and suspends momentarily, seven feet high. Catches bubbles blown by OLD MAN. Waves frantically. Falls to trampoline. Jumps to floor. Looks up at OLD MAN.

Gets on trampoline. Bounces higher. Waves frantically. Does backflip. Waves frantically. Reaches apex of jump and suspends momentarily, eight feet high. Waves frantically. Falls to trampoline. Jumps to floor. Looks up at OLD MAN. Waves, not so frantically.

Sits on edge of trampoline. Fifteen seconds. Stands up. Looks up at OLD MAN. Takes off harness, places it on trampoline. Sits on floor. Looks up at OLD MAN. Looks at harness. Walks around stage, returns to harness. Sits on trampoline. Looks up at OLD MAN. Waves, not so frantically.

OLD MAN waves and levitates up and out of sight.

Rope descends, suspended four feet high.

YOUNG MAN puts on harness. Gets on trampoline. Bounces. Grabs rope. Suspends.

Rope, with YOUNG MAN attached, falls to trampoline. YOUNG MAN jumps to floor. Stores rope beneath trampoline.

Another rope descends, suspended six feet high.

YOUNG MAN gets on trampoline. Bounces. Grabs rope. Suspends.

Rope, with YOUNG MAN attached, falls to trampoline. YOUNG MAN jumps to floor. Stores rope beneath trampoline.

Another rope descends, suspended seven feet high.

YOUNG MAN gets on trampoline. Bounces. Grabs rope. Suspends.

CURTAIN.

San Francisco Poems
(1999)

#1

A new leather jacket
trampolining rain
to the street
and how my blue eyes
stand out here among
crowded Chinese faces.
Smells of food cooking and decaying
and I am finally here but here is not home but here
is San Francisco a place of holy wars
preservation of the spirit
through words through shoes
through mixed media /multitimbral
and unforgiving,
There is a new race rising up from our streets
barriers dropping
like hurdles kicked over by
the loser of the race
wars that characterize our polarized
consciousness.
Oh yes it may take awhile, but ride the MUNI
and look into her eyes if she'll let you.
Stand in the void if you know how to access it –
And Listen.

And the dim refrain
of the song of unity – and song that will not stand still,
grips me faintly through the rain and the Chinese,
pulsing my meridians, setting me silently aflame.

But do not mistake silence for boredom,
for I am harmonizing with Love.

I am merely listening.

13 Feb 1999
4:23 PM

Marin Dream in B♭

#2

Jade green
and opaque
she stands
in the
vestibule
of my oversoul
She is Transmigration
Blessed Gatekeeper
Sliding
in
    and
        out
of deity
She is one 2 be gifted
with all sincerity
and
I
can
not

b r e a k

the

silence.

13 Feb 1999
4:54 PM
San Francisco

#3

Decompression chamber
smokeless and sacrosanct
I come to you devoid of philosophy,
mute and pensive, housing a resident alien --
I think he is a Zen Master, mindless and mindful,
and like a raft upon a pool or a pond in a drizzle, I sizzle.
> the intensity of his clarity
> the clarity of his intention.
But then again maybe he is retarded,
born to be led from innocence
into the nightmares
of his caretakers.

Let me stretch my legs my arms my back
and acclimate
to this gravity
this planet with no
history to share, no
unity to strive for, for it
sees itself
> only
> in terms of
itself.

In Pan-galactic moments I can see hope,
my own projection, perhaps,
like a laser boring holes
in Pacific waves
crashing on Tennessee Valley sand.

13 Feb 1999
5:53 PM
San Francisco

#4

This rainy morning I
shed invisible tears
in my coffee I
write imaginary symphonies I
stare across the table
to the chair you occupied yesterday I
trace the wickerwork in delicate
lattices until finally I
come to my senses and
remember that Valentine's Day
is a Hallmark holiday, and not
one that means a thing to either of us.

I take a deep breath, sigh,
and add an uncharacteristic
spoonful of sugar to my coffee.

I am calm, disjointed,
and far from home.

14 Feb 1999
8:29 AM
San Francisco

*"Marin Dream in Bb for Flute and Piano" came to life
in the Bay Area during that weekend in February, 1999.
Sketched by hand, polished and printed with Finale.*

Internal Medicine
(2000)

Internal Medicine

Portal Poem, Saturday, October 3	145
What the Messenger Said	146
Carolyn's Song	148
Magnetic Poems	150
tonight I am eating chicken	151
Adel's Take On Modeling	153
Lunch Poem, June 18	154
Leaving Long Island	156
Alzheimer's	157
House D	158
In Response to Ani	159
Epiphany	160
Socorro	162
Almost Mother-in-law (fiction)	164
Obligatory Y2K Poem	177

Portal Poem, Saturday, October 3

It is the kind of Saturday
       where worry would be foolish
  Gingerbread houses
             standing on these mountains,
     splendid in their transience.

I come here to remember, to peer
       into the pre-dawn sky and be humbled.

It is the kind of morning that takes all afternoon.
       A certain suspension of time welcomes me,
           unfolds me in her arms.
       "You are safe," she whispers. "You are eternal."
  I do not respond, I just let her
       rock me in her hyperdimensional ocean.

As if pulled by magnets under my feet I
       return to the mountain view, slightly
  sloped roofs overhanging picture windows.
       I think of Holland, though I've
         never been there, and of your blue eyes
trembling, not daring to let me in.

       But it is the kind of Saturday
           where regret would be foolish.
  What Is is what you make of it,
       and All That Is is all that you co-create.

       But through the parallax of your paradox
           you can not yet bring yourself to be
  Honest, and in love with Love.

And I, star-born, ride on, sailing off with the next gust of wind.

What the Messenger Said

Break free
of that cluster of crystals
your brothers and sisters
all of your worldly concerns
Step out from the violence
and into the silence
and remember your karma returns

Remember Atlantis and the science you wrought
the monsters you created
Remember the earth is just one family
and everyone is related

Remember Tibet and the way that you chanted
the silent vows you took

A sound filled the air with sweet harmonics
and the walls slowly faded away
the angel appeared in luminous light
and showed me how to pray
Pray not for yourself, nor your personal wants
worry not for your personal needs
pray for the earth, the sweet crying Earth
and all the people she feeds
"Who are you?" I asked/to the luminous sphere
with a mix of excitement and trembling fear

He said "I am your angel, and my name I'll reveal
when I see that you're ready to reach out and feel
for all that existed and all that remains
and all of the joy that the cosmos contains"

I was blissful with rapture and I opened my eyes
the angel remained, to my surprise
His wings were like cotton, his hair was pure white
And I've never forgotten his tranquil white light.

Carolyn's Song

A calm sobriety
      has pervaded your voice
And so soon after contact initial.

And I could be free
      of desire
      of the essence of time
I could make you my Muse and move on.
Spirit has given me new eyes to see
      and a new body to face this new day.

The sunrise was cloudy -- impenterable mystery
      There is so much we can not see.

And Today will not be like yesterday
      And will I ever see you again?

Last night I dreamed of my childhood
      And all I could never see
           And the sunrise awoke me
           And the angels invoked me
           And I went for a walk outside.

Sweet isolation/the lessons of Saturn
      A time to forgive and retreat
           I'm charting the seasons
           forgiving my treasons
           Becoming a child of light.

Was it not Spirit that brought us together?
  Is it not me, disconnected, sentimental?

I came to you, revealed myself
        then duty called and I flew.
    And now I sit at God's behest and
        wonder what you'll do.

10 Mar 96
7:14 AM
Taos, NM

Magnetic Poems – For T

#1

Other children crave chocolate
She wants twilight's blue foreplay
a marriage of spirit and cliché
Juvenile voodoo, a dream of Timbuktu
Anatomy and reason were never enough

#2

Some psychiatrists won't reconcile
loyalty with sublime smiles
    "Take Me There Take Me" she whispered
in delicate pentameter on his birthday,
her cartoon passion lovelier than winter rhyme.

And you want a versatile knight to
    father your risqué appetites each afternoon?
So my dearest
    is it kindred spirit
        body sex
            or
a prance through beautiful black moonwater
and no guarantee?

tonight I am eating chicken
wearing lazy clothes and cleaning the house

tonight I am eating chicken
transmuting the fear of the masses

Popocatepetl gave her first warnings this week.
sounds like Gaia's due in 1998

give the sweet chant give her the
blessed om rise and shine

the great transition is here is now is continual evolution

tonight I eat chicken
for the dark brothers giving themselves
to the reformation
for those in africa with aids
in america with aids
for the people who shop in department stores
timidly checking labels.
for latina angels working at taco bell

people clouded/enshrouded by visions and viruses
awake arise the great opening-up is upon us.

multitimbral geometries

ascend attune listen closely yes there are some
who are here to succumb

there will be viruses there will be plagues there will be the
heartbeats of children rising from the new earth
singing her praises.

tonight I am eating chicken

for the 1,200,000 chickens
and probably more slaughtered in hong kong --

and because I could not eat beef when her majesty
slaughtered her mad cows.

tonight I am eating chicken because so many can not.

Albuquerque
30 Dec 1997 02:28

Adel's Take On Modeling

"I had a chance to model," I said,
     "but it kind of fell through."
"Why, because you wouldn't show them your gruben?"

Lunch Poem – June 18

Sang Karaoke in Brooklyn last night
    running on New York water,
        quadriceps sore.
    Old friends, Brian, Adam,
        hometown accents fill subway cars.
    Definitely don't miss that subterranean stench,
fetid rush hour, Auschwitz-style on the 6 train uptown.

In the City of Death it takes $30 a day to fill my belly, to
    keep me hydrated –
    drinking water at $1.79 a liter will drain the
pockets quickly.
    Though I must admit to liking my
    Madison Avenue temp job.

And though I'm no adrenaline junkie I can see how
millions crave the Rave, but at what cost?
A thousand or more for a womb with a view?

I think now of my sanctum, sweet Albuquerque,
    my stupefaction there, and my inability to write.
There, I do it all telepathically. But here, I
    walk amongst the throngs, displaced,
    a traveler returning home, instinctively scanning
    crowds for familiar faces, finding none.

And it's almost better this way, for what is my
    connection here?
    Parents, old friends, who know me for who I was,
untrained, unmanifest.

Stevie in his infinite inner vision resounds in my ears –
    "you're the only one who sees
        the changes you put yourself through.
        So don't you worry 'bout a thing!"

Girls making my eyes pop out,
    some confident & brazen, some
    just pretending. And I, whimsically,
worry about my soulmate across the sea.

And all this hardly matters as I step to the Eternal Now,
    heart ablaze,
    almost comfortable in a body.
    Loose ends, like jazz progressions,
will eventually resolve,
    and I will eventually go home.

But for now I pulse to a Gemini beat,
    may the light and life shine through me.

18 June 1998
12:24 PM, NYC

Leaving Long Island

A heavy calm,
firm & indisputable
fills the one o'clock hour.
Silent triumph in my heart
decriminalized, finally.

Day turns to night and not
a thought fills my head.
Sleep is deep and dreamless.

And I, foggy and serene, stare
into yesterday and forgive.

1 July 1998
1:18 AM

ALZHEIMER'S

She spits lightning at walls of an apartment
    she hardly knows
    Names are lost
    Numbers make no sense.
WHO ARE ALL THESE PEOPLE?
She held me once when I was small
    She is me/where I'll wind up
        when winter waltzes
            across my palm.
The nurses say she could live five more years.

I say her walls need new memories
for she no longer knows where she was.

for my grandmother,
Goldie Davis (1908-1998)

House D
for Brian

A child of mud arises from the desert floor
eyes willing and ears open
coyote wails from somewhere behind the mesa
dogs in packs harmonize in response.
Child is one of seven in the
two-bedroom rivershack
Mom Dad Grandma Grandpa make
eleven in total.
The smell of bonfire & beans and
distant Spanish screaming find
me and Lawrence
sitting, smoking on the porch.

In Response to Ani

*If no one's watching
you are free
to exercise
sweet autonomy
extract your sweet
vibrational essence
and like a dandelion in the wind
flutter to indeterminate
predetermined
destinations.*

*If no one's watching
you are free
to exercise
sweet anarchy
invent your evolved
sovereign enclaves
and like an insect in the jet stream
spread your sweet fertile song.*

*If no one's watching
you are free
to doubt
the existence of deity,
though this seems to me
trite and inefficient.*

*If no one's watching
then every star in the sky
is a liar twinkling
through eternity.*

Epiphany

Has it really been 18 months
mute, transfixed,
metacognition on hyperdrive?
The eddies of time
        swirl around me and laugh
                at my grasping,
                        my three-quarter surrender.

Since puberty I have been dropping,
        slowly, into this body
                like the boy growing into his father's shoes –
        Shoes of Jews on postcards
                of Holocaust atrocities
                        and somewhere I cellularly remember
                            that camp
                                those guards
                                      that horror.

And here I am, stationed in the land of mañana and
as the stars dance over my awning I inhale and buzz
to the spectacle that my folly has become.
All that moving
        packing and unpacking
        sifting and shifting like water through coffee grinds
all that running
        and not a medal to show for it

Cataleptic and cynical I began
        watchful and perspicacious I have become –
And now, just past aphelion, yet not quite returning,
        I sit and stare, the infant learning
                that there are restitutions
                only Time can make - and not
                      every ounce of your attention can
                          grease the larger wheel.

A small victory, perhaps, but one to cherish.

Socorro

I awoke to your poetry this morning --
        your voice like Nicaraguan coffee,
                and immediately began to write

There is no verbal translation for molecular transformation
        so I have remained silent,
        waiting
        for you to ask the next question.

"Are you aware how much I want you, *gringuito*?"

And you,
        ojos de chocolate
        labios de carmesi
continue your march
head before heart
second chakra aflame
        into the murky infinite possibility

And my star car is hitched to a silver cord
        and the only wisdom I have learned
        is to get out of its way --
to trust a future vaster than my current genetic
structure can comprehend

So I sit regally in the plush seats of my chariot and
quaff from the liquid movie,
        carefully choosing my roles.

Your chocolate desire
        semi-sweet and
        microcosmically temporal.
If only you could sit patiently like the Enlightened One
        debajo de los juniperos
and let my sweet androgyny
        take you
        remake you

Look closer before you judge me --
        nail me up on some false wooden memory
        for I have come through time repeatedly
and so have you

escorpion luminosa
cazadora anhelosa

You take advantage of my infantile Spanish
    I can not understand the words you whisper
    I can only translate into raw emotion.
When will you realize, *chuparrosa*,
    that we are already united,
and from there the celestial symphony urges us on --
    "Work, if you dare."

Stand back -- look honestly with the eyes of a witness
    and you will see
        how inadequate
            the translation
    from light
        and sound
into English
    can be.

Almost Mother-in-law

It was the July after my grandfather was committed and our rent was six days overdue. She was cramping so I got her some Ayurvedic tea. But her mood had been sullen for about three weeks now, and even I knew this was more than your average PMS. Liza and I had been through our share of troubles. Her parents hate me. Classic story. Her parents met me when I was in a minimum-hygiene phase, and at 19, still grappling with parental and societal expectations. My parents still wanted me to be a doctor or a lawyer, and her parents wanted me to be somewhere else, anywhere but around and in their oldest and only daughter. Her mom wore her hair straight and short, her make-up bronze and brazen. She was mildly phobic, never driving alone and always leaving a radio on when she left the house. By the time her mother became my mortal enemy -- a goddess I had slain lifetimes ago -- the engagement was already official. I really believed back then that genetics had nothing to do with it. Her dad wore Jordache jeans on the weekends and worked as a prison guard in the Bronx -- or at least that's what he called it. He was dean of a high school and he's pretty good with a knife. He liked me a little more than Liza's mom did, but not much.

The Goldsmiths were very typically Long Island Jewish. Liza's parents were middle-class and deeply committed to their children. My family was middle-class Jewish as well, but we had moved to Long Island from New Orleans, and our values were never quite the same. I thought her parents were too absorbed in the way they looked and the car they drove, and her parents thought I was a perpetual underachiever who could never make their daughter happy – which, at the time, was probably true. I was in quite an existentialist phase back then, writing a lot and belonging to various poetic and civil action groups, most of which just stayed up late and got stoned under the pretense of societal reformation via poetic revolution. I was not shaving much, showering occasionally, and having a lot of fun.

I'll never forget the look in Liza's grandmother's eye when I showed up on Liza's arm for a cousin's wedding. Her look was a mixture of revolt and personal failure. I dolefully grew accustomed to these cherished family events, where Liza would leave me with her relatives to talk about money or sports and vanish with her mother and grandmother for "conferences," the nature of which I was not privy to. But Liza would always come out of these pep talks with an air of infinite superiority and wouldn't let me sleep with her for three days. One such memorable occasion came to pass at her cousin's son's bris, in the suburbs in New Jersey. I was discussing my personal uses of ginseng and ginger with her uncle, who was complaining about having low energy, when her mother, who hadn't even heard the beginning of the conversation, snarled from behind a mastectomy, "Herbs don't work. Drugs work." She had hissed so loud that conversation temporarily stopped. All eyes gathered around Liza's mother and I, eyes locked, hers in anger and resentment and mine in cartoon bewilderment. Into this silence I offered an unfriendly, "How would you know? Have you used herbs as part of your treatment?"

"How dare you talk about my treatment!" her mother hissed, and stormed out of the room. I looked at Liza standing defiantly next to her grandmother and knew I had no support. I looked at Liza and said, "Can you catch a ride home? I'm not welcome here. I'm leaving." Fast forward to the aforementioned July. Liza was working at a health food store in Boulder, having visions of New York every day, regretting my decision to leave a decent-paying entry-level job and a relatively inexpensive apartment on the Upper East Side. In the morning I'd roll over and Liza would do an inward sneer, a technique she'd perfected with much practice. She had reached a point in her practice where she could actually structure a smile to conduct the undercurrents of fear and anger through our auric field. They teach that in Boulder. Weekend workshops.

    I was working in Longmont as a DD case manager and part-time in Boulder at retirement homes. We were renting a cute little house near Pearl Street, but Liza was never truly happy. She would make little comments about the porch, or bitch when the gas bill came. She watched TV more and more and stayed up late with me less and less. One Thursday night that summer, over sake and sushi, at a little restaurant we both know and love, I ask her if she's happy here. She says she likes Boulder, and that for the first time since leaving home she feels like she's making something of herself, and doing things the way she likes to. There's a glow in her face I haven't seen in months, and I know she's telling the truth. I drink a little more sake with my unagi and we go home and make love.

    That night I have a dream about Liza's mother in rollers waking us up and asking us to make breakfast, and put the cats outside (we don't have cats) because she's allergic. She complained about the omelet I made and wondered aloud whether her daughter had made the right choice. In this dream I happened to have a plasma gun, and I disintegrated her right there in the kitchen.

    I woke up and knew something was seriously wrong. Liza was still sleeping so I got dressed and took Duke out for a walk, basking in the post-dawn quiet and the morning sun, deliberating where and when I should talk to Liza about my dream; whether I should mention it at all. I let Duke off the leash and retrace history. A little over two years ago, her parents came to see us, this only two months after we moved to Boulder. I'd never seen an umbilical cord with such elasticity. I asked Liza for the address of the factory that makes them. She slapped me.

When they arrived they had us meet them at their hotel. There was no way her mother was going to actually come to the house -- that might mean acknowledging that I do still exist and I do still screw her daughter. Her father was a little bit more hip about it. Eventually he asked about the house, and persuaded his wife to come see it. But something about his demeanor always annoyed me. He spoke very loud, and had one of those dinky ponytails and no hair on his legs. But you still have to admire a man who patrols hallways lined with firearms. Or question his sanity.

They took Liza and I to an Italian restaurant and Liza's Dad ordered from the wine list. We were chowing garlic bread and sipping chianti, being generally civil. Her parents always did have great taste in restaurants, and her father always knew exactly what to order. Going out to dinner was definitely the highlight of spending time with Liza's parents. "What are you doing for a living?" her mother asked (as if she didn't already know) with her typical I'm-an-older-and-more-established-Jew-than-you undertones. I looked at Liza as if to say "Why is she doing this again?" But Liza stared back defiantly as if she had asked the question herself.

My heart sank, briefly. I hadn't seen the Goldsmiths for almost two years, and in this absence the similarities between Liza and her mother seemed to grow. In the dim light, as I sat across from Liza and next to her mother, the similarities between the two were striking. Liza definitely looked more like her Dad, but the more either woman spoke, the more the likeness stood out. It was finally dawning on me where Liza picked up her technique. In that moment I knew I was going for broke. Either this umbilical cord was going to snap or I was. I took a gulp of chianti and responded. "I've been working with old folks, and handicapped folks. I commute to Longmont 4 times a week. It's about 20 minutes from here. And you know I'm a writer and a musician. I'm starting my M.F.A. in the fall."

"You can't make any money working with old folks," Mrs. G sneered. I should have reminded her that she works only part-time and is on her third mortgage, but this time I wanted to see things to their logical conclusion. "And what do you do nowadays?" Liza's mother turned to her father and sent him a cocked eyebrow. He quickly changed the subject, talking about Liza's relatives and recent family events. The Italian food was spectacular. I ate in silence. Though the karmic resolution between Mrs G and myself was avoided for one more day, the rest of the meal was generally pleasant, with me reveling in the food and Liza catching up with her parents. I stayed out of their way for the remainder of their visit to Boulder.

***

I got home this warm July morning, the morning after the plasma gun dream, to Liza cooking breakfast, looking cheerful and hungry. I wondered whether people who slept together shared dreams or dream fragments, and decided that they probably did. But to Liza the monster that I blew away with a plasma gun could have been Mr. Rogers or some other well-disguised demon. I kissed her good morning and sat in my chair, sipping the orange juice she poured for me, taking in smells of her eggs & spices. I kissed the back of right shoulder, on the place where she always wanted a tattoo and I always opposed. I bet she's got one now.

She turned and gave me a hug. "Where'd you go with Duke?" "We went to Chatauqua Park. I let him run." "Want to hike this weekend? It's been awhile." "Love to." She kissed my cheek. "Sit